SAVORY SOUPS & SALADS

SAVORY SOUPS & SALADS

Frank R. Blenn

American Diabetes Association

| *Publisher* | *Editorial Director* | *Managing Editor* |
| Susan H. Lau | Peter Banks | Christine Welch |

| *Assistant Managing Editor* | *Associate Editor* |
| Laurie Guffey | Sherrye Landrum |

Printed in the United States of America
99 98 97 96 95 94   10 9 8 7 6 5 4 3 2 1

American Diabetes Association
1660 Duke Street
Alexandria, VA 22314

Page design and typesetting services by Insight Graphics, Inc.
Cover design by Wickham & Associates, Inc.

Library of Congress Cataloging-in-Publication Data

Blenn, Frank R., 1963-
Savory soups & salads / Frank R. Blenn.
p. cm. — (Healthy selects)
Includes index.
ISBN 0-945448-41-4 (pbk.) : $8.95
1. Diabetes—Diet therapy—Recipes. 2. Soups. 3. Salads.
I. Title. II. Title: Savory soups and salads. III. Series.
RC662.B598 1994
641.8' 13—dc20   94-24479 CIP

CONTENTS

FOREWORD

The American Diabetes Association is proud to announce *Healthy Selects,* a new cookbook series dedicated to the premise that light, healthy food can be good for you *and* taste great, too. *Savory Soups & Salads,* the third book in the series, is a collection of easy-to-prepare soup and salad recipes you can serve at elegant parties or comfortable family dinners. Each recipe has American Diabetes Association-approved exchanges and all nutritional information provided. We know you'll enjoy the new ways to serve some of your favorite foods, as well as the unique ideas found in the series.

Author Frank Blenn created these recipes to help others cope with diabetes, and thought to offer them to us in an effort to reach and assist a wider audience. We deeply appreciate his generosity. The Association owes a special debt of gratitude to Madelyn L. Wheeler, MS, RD, CDE, and her company, Nutritional Computing Concepts, for the thorough and careful preparation of nutritional calculations and exchange information. Ms. Wheeler offered many valuable suggestions through each step of the book production process. Robyn Webb Associates conducted taste-testing on every recipe and ensured the accuracy and quality of the finished product. Ms. Webb also developed many of the recipes in this book.

The original manuscript was reviewed by Karmeen Kulkarni, MS, RD, CDE, and Madelyn Wheeler, MS, RD, CDE. The final manuscript was reviewed by Sue McLaughlin, RD, CDE. Patty Walsh provided creative illustrations for each title in the series.

Have fun adding variety and zest to your diet with the *Healthy Selects* Series!

American Diabetes Association

PREFACE

Savory Soups & Salads is the third cookbook in a new series offering lighter and healthier recipes that still taste wonderful. I served many of these recipes, with great success, at elegant parties and casual dinners. I know you will appreciate the abundance of ways to serve the delicious recipes presented in this series.

My long-term goal was to write and share the results with you. With that in mind, I would like to offer my warmest and most sincere appreciation to the American Diabetes Association in helping me reach my goal. Without their interest and assistance, this series of books would just be another manuscript in my office.

I would like to dedicate this book to my family, who encouraged me to find a wider audience, and to my close friends (who are never without their opinions!) for taste-testing their way through many joyful times.

I hope you enjoy these delicious additions to a varied and healthy diet.

Frank R. Blenn

INTRODUCTION

Packed with tasty and easy-to-prepare recipes for soups and salads, *Savory Soups & Salads* is a terrific addition to your cookbook library. There are some important points to keep in mind, however, as you try all the recipes:

◆ The nutrient analysis section *only includes* the ingredients listed in the ingredients section! The nutrient analyses do *not* include serving suggestions sometimes provided in other sections of the recipe. For example, in the recipe for Parmesan Dressing, we suggest that you serve it over green beans or asparagus. But, because green beans or asparagus are not included as ingredients, you know that the nutrient analysis only applies to the Parmesan Dressing recipe itself. Similarly, suggested garnishes are not included in the analyses, unless they appear in the ingredients list.

◆ In general, we have suggested using olive oil instead of low-calorie margarine. You can use low-calorie margarine if you prefer, depending on your individual goals. Olive oil provides more monounsaturated fats, which are healthier, but low-calorie margarine does contain fewer calories. Feel free to interchange them if you need to.

◆ If you can find a version of an ingredient lower in fat than the low-fat items we used, feel free to use it instead. The recipes will still work, and your total fat grams will go down slightly. We usually use low-fat options, defined as containing 3 grams of fat or less per serving. When we use the term low-calorie, that means 40 calories or less per serving. Lite soy sauce is lower in sodium than regular soy sauce. When we say a dash of salt, that's 1/16 of a teaspoon.

◆ Remember that when a food is listed as a Free Food, there may still be limits on the serving size. For example, for many dressings and toppings, only 2 Tbsp. or less is free. More than that and the food has an exchange value. Also, in terms of nutrient values, 1 Starch/Bread Exchange can be interchanged with 1 Fruit Exchange.

◆ The nutrient analyses provided for the soup stock recipes have been calculated based on canned, low-sodium chicken or beef broth. This is because the calculations can vary based on individual straining techniques and vegetables used. Finally, note that the serving sizes in these recipes are not uniform, and vary from recipe to recipe.

Good luck, and we hope you enjoy *Savory Soups & Salads!*

HEARTY STEWS & CHOWDERS

QUICK SHRIMP GUMBO

4 servings/serving size: 3 oz. shrimp with sauce and 1/4 cup rice

- 2 cups canned tomatoes, undrained
- 1/4 cup chopped green pepper
- 1 medium onion, chopped
- 1 cup uncooked white rice
- 1/2 cup low-sodium chicken broth
- 1 medium garlic clove, minced
- Dash hot pepper sauce (Tabasco)
- Fresh ground pepper
- 12 oz. precooked jumbo shrimp

1. Place all the ingredients except the shrimp in a large stockpot and bring to a boil. Reduce the heat, cover, and let simmer for 25 to 30 minutes.
2. Add the shrimp, cover, and simmer for 5 to 10 minutes or until shrimp is thoroughly heated. Serve hot.

Lean Meat Exchange 1	Cholesterol . . . . 167 milligrams
Starch/Bread Exchange 1	Total Carbohydrate . . . . 21 grams
Vegetable Exchange 1	Dietary Fiber . . . . 2 grams
Calories 182	Sugars . . . . 6 grams
Total Fat . . . . 2 grams	Protein . . . . 21 grams
Saturated Fat . . . . 0 grams	Sodium . . . . 396 milligrams
Calories from fat 14	

CHICKEN AND MUSHROOM SOUP

6 servings/serving size: 1 cup

*T*ry *serving this soup with fresh Buttermilk Biscuits (see recipe, page 29).*

- 1/2 lb. boneless, skinless chicken breast, cubed
- 1 quart low-sodium chicken broth
- 1 Tbsp. lite soy sauce
- 1 cup sliced mushrooms, stems removed
- 1 Tbsp. finely chopped scallions
- 1 Tbsp. dry sherry

1. Cube the chicken and set aside. Add the chicken broth, soy sauce, mushrooms, scallions, and sherry to a soup pot. Simmer the soup for 10 minutes.
2. Add the chicken cubes and simmer for 6 to 8 minutes more. Serve with additional soy sauce if desired (but be aware that this will raise the sodium level of the soup!).

. . . .

Lean Meat Exchange	1	Cholesterol	24 milligrams
Vegetable Exchange	1	Total Carbohydrate	2 grams
Calories	74	Dietary Fiber	0 grams
Total Fat	2 grams	Sugars	1 gram
Saturated Fat	1 gram	Protein	10 grams
Calories from fat	19	Sodium	159 milligrams

POTATO CHOWDER

8 servings/serving size: 1 cup

This is a creamy, low-fat version of a potato lover's favorite!

- ♦ 2 tsp. olive oil
- ♦ 3/4 cup chopped onion
- ♦ 1/2 cup diced celery
- ♦ 1 bay leaf
- ♦ 1 clove garlic, minced
- ♦ 1/4 cup flour
- ♦ 1/4 cup evaporated skim milk
- ♦ 2 cups skim milk
- ♦ 3-1/2 cups low-sodium chicken broth
- ♦ 1-1/2 lb. potatoes, peeled and cut into 2-inch cubes
- ♦ 1 tsp. salt (optional)
- ♦ 1 tsp. dried basil
- ♦ 1/4 tsp. dried thyme
- ♦ 1/4 tsp. nutmeg
- ♦ 1/4 tsp. celery seeds
- ♦ Fresh ground pepper
- ♦ 1 Tbsp. cider vinegar
- ♦ 1 Tbsp. minced parsley

1. In a large saucepan, heat the oil. Add the onion, celery and bay leaf; cook over medium heat for 5 minutes, stirring occasionally.
2. Add garlic and slowly add the flour; mix well. Slowly add the evaporated milk, skim milk and chicken broth. Bring to a boil, stirring constantly.
3. Add the potatoes, salt, basil, thyme, nutmeg, celery seeds and pepper. Reduce the heat and let simmer, uncovered, for 25 to 30 minutes or until potatoes are tender, stirring frequently.
4. Add the vinegar and discard the bay leaf. Remove 3 cups of the mixture and place in a food processor; puree. Add the mixture back to the soup pot and mix thoroughly. Sprinkle with parsley and serve.

••

Starch/Bread Exchange	1-1/2	Total Carbohydrate	23 grams
Calories	133	Dietary Fiber	2 grams
Total Fat	2 grams	Sugars	6 grams
Saturated Fat	0 grams	Protein	6 grams
Calories from fat	19	Sodium	342 milligrams
Cholesterol	2 milligrams	w/o added salt	75 milligrams

OLD-FASHIONED VEGETABLE BEEF STEW

8 servings/serving size: 1 cup

Loaded with chunky vegetables, this stew will warm you up on a cold day!

- 1 lb. lean beef for stew, cut into 1-inch cubes
- 2 Tbsp. olive oil
- 1 medium onion, diced
- 2 garlic cloves, crushed
- 28 oz. canned tomatoes, slightly crushed
- 2 cups low-sodium beef broth
- 2 large carrots, peeled and cut into 1/4-inch round slices
- 1/2 lb. mushrooms, sliced
- 1/2 lb. green beans, cut into 2-inch pieces
- 4 celery stalks, sliced diagonally
- Fresh black pepper
- Dash cayenne pepper
- Dash hot pepper sauce (Tabasco)
- 2 medium russet or white potatoes, peeled, cut into 1-inch cubes

1. In a large saucepan over medium heat, lightly brown the meat in the olive oil. Add the onion, garlic, tomatoes, and beef broth; bring to a boil.
2. Reduce to a simmer; add carrots, mushrooms, green beans, and celery. Season the soup with pepper, cayenne pepper, and hot pepper sauce. Cover and simmer for 45 minutes to 1 hour.
3. Add the potatoes and cook until tender, adding water if necessary. Serve hot.

....

Lean Meat Exchange	1	Calories from fat 64
Starch/Bread Exchange	1	Cholesterol .... 33 milligrams
Vegetable Exchange	1	Total Carbohydrate .... 20 grams
Fat Exchange	1/2	Dietary Fiber .... 4 grams
Calories	193	Sugars .... 7 grams
Total Fat	7 grams	Protein .... 14 grams
Saturated Fat	2 grams	Sodium .... 250 milligrams

ENGLISH BEEF STEW

8 servings/serving size: 1 cup

This stew has a slightly different flavor than Old-Fashioned Vegetable Beef Stew, but is just as satisfying.

- 2 lb. lean beef for stew, cut into large chunks
- 1-1/2 Tbsp. flour
- 2 Tbsp. canola oil
- 2 cups boiling water
- 2 tsp. garlic powder
- 1 Tbsp. Worcestershire sauce
- Dash salt and pepper
- 1 large yellow onion, quartered
- 4 large carrots, peeled and quartered
- 3 medium potatoes, white or russet, cut into 1-inch cubes
- 1 cup canned stewed tomatoes

1. Roll the beef cubes in the flour. In a large saucepan over medium heat, heat the canola oil. Add the beef and saute a few pieces of beef at a time. When all beef has been browned, add the boiling water to the pan.
2. Add the garlic powder, Worcestershire sauce, salt, and pepper. Lower the heat, cover, and let simmer for 2 to 2-1/2 hours or until the meat is very tender.
3. Add the onion, carrots, potatoes, and tomatoes. Let simmer 30 minutes until all vegetables are tender. Transfer to a serving bowl and serve.

....

Lean Meat Exchange	3	Cholesterol	65 milligrams
Starch/Bread Exchange	1	Total Carbohydrate	20 grams
Calories	256	Dietary Fiber	3 grams
Total Fat	9 grams	Sugars	7 grams
Saturated Fat	2 grams	Protein	23 grams
Calories from fat	82	Sodium	183 milligrams

CHICKEN STEW
WITH NOODLES

8 servings/serving size: 1 cup stew and 1/2 cup cooked noodles

*T*ry *using this stew to top rice or a baked potato, too.*

- 1 Tbsp. olive oil
- 1 onion, chopped
- 2 garlic cloves, minced
- 1 lb. boneless, skinless chicken breast, cubed
- 2 Tbsp. flour
- 3 cups low-sodium chicken broth

- 1 cup dry white wine
- 1 Tbsp. chopped fresh thyme (or 1 tsp. dried)
- 1/2 cup minced parsley
- 1 lb. cooked noodles, hot

1. In a large saucepan, saute the onion and garlic in the oil for about 5 minutes. Add the chicken cubes and saute until chicken is cooked (about 10 minutes).
2. Sprinkle the flour over the chicken. Add the chicken broth, wine, and thyme. Bring to a boil, then lower the heat, and simmer for 30 minutes.
3. Toss together the noodles and the parsley. Pour the stew over the noodles and serve.

••

Lean Meat Exchange	2	Cholesterol	53 milligrams
Starch/Bread Exchange	1	Total Carbohydrate	19 grams
Calories	191	Dietary Fiber	1 gram
Total Fat	5 grams	Sugars	3 grams
Saturated Fat	1 gram	Protein	17 grams
Calories from fat	42	Sodium	58 milligrams

CHICKEN AND YAM STEW

12 servings/serving size: about 1 cup with 3–4 ounces chicken

Serve fresh, crusty bread with this hearty stew—rich in Vitamin A!

- 1/4 cup flour
- 1 tsp. salt (optional)
- 3 lb. boneless, skinless chicken breast, cubed
- 2 Tbsp. olive oil
- 2 Tbsp. chopped onion
- 2 cups low-sodium chicken broth
- 1/4 cup dry white wine
- 1-1/2 lb. yams
- 1 lb. green beans, sliced
- 2 cups sliced celery

1. Combine the flour and salt, shake the chicken pieces in the flour and set aside. Heat the olive oil in a large skillet. Add the chicken pieces and brown on all sides.
2. Move the chicken pieces to one side, add the onions, and cook until tender. Add the chicken broth and wine to the skillet, cover and let simmer for 30 minutes.
3. Peel and quarter the yams. Add the yams, green beans, and celery to the skillet. Cover and continue simmering for 25 to 30 minutes or until vegetables are tender.

....

Lean Meat Exchange 3	Total Carbohydrate . . . . 19 grams
Starch/Bread Exchange 1	Dietary Fiber . . . . 3 grams
Calories 241	Sugars . . . . 1 gram
Total Fat . . . . 6 grams	Protein . . . . 27 grams
Saturated Fat . . . . 1 gram	Sodium . . . . 267 milligrams
Calories from fat 50	w/o added salt 89
Cholesterol . . . . 69 milligrams	

FRESH FISH STEW

6 servings/serving size: 1 cup

You can use almost any fish in this stew—we've suggested halibut.

- 2 Tbsp. olive oil
- 1 large garlic clove, minced
- 1 small onion, chopped
- 1 large green pepper, chopped
- 1 lb. crushed tomatoes
- 1 Tbsp. tomato paste
- 1/2 tsp. dried basil
- 1/2 tsp. dried oregano
- 1/4 cup dry red wine
- Dash salt and pepper
- 1/2 cup uncooked white rice
- 1/2 lb. fresh halibut, cubed
- 2 Tbsp. chopped parsley

1. Heat the olive oil in a 3-quart saucepan. Add the garlic, onion, and green pepper; saute for 10 minutes over low heat until vegetables are tender.
2. Add the tomatoes, tomato paste, basil, oregano, wine, salt, and pepper. Let simmer for 15 minutes. Add the rice and continue to cook for 15 minutes.
3. Add the halibut and cook for about 5 to 7 minutes until fish is cooked through. Garnish stew with chopped parsley and serve.

••

Medium-Fat Meat Exchange 1	Cholesterol .... 12 milligrams
Starch/Bread Exchange 1	Total Carbohydrate .... 22 grams
Vegetable Exchange 1	Dietary Fiber .... 2 grams
Calories 181	Sugars .... 5 grams
Total Fat .... 6 grams	Protein .... 10 grams
Saturated Fat .... 1 gram	Sodium .... 72 milligrams
Calories from fat 52	

QUICK MANHATTAN CLAM CHOWDER

8 servings/serving size: about 1 cup

Try serving this chunky chowder with hot sourdough bread.

- 3 medium carrots, peeled and chopped coarsely
- 3 large white or russet potatoes, peeled and chopped coarsely
- 4 celery stalks, chopped coarsely
- 2-1/2 cups minced clams, drained
- 2 cups canned tomatoes, slightly crushed
- 1 Tbsp. imitation bacon bits (optional)
- 1/2 tsp. dried thyme or 1 tsp. minced fresh thyme
- Dash salt and pepper

Add all the ingredients to a large soup pot. Cover and let simmer for 1 to 2 hours. Serve hot.

....

Lean Meat Exchange 1	Total Carbohydrate . . . . 23 grams
Starch/Bread Exchange 1-1/2	Dietary Fiber . . . . 3 grams
Calories 161	Sugars . . . . 7 grams
Total Fat . . . . 1 gram	Protein . . . . 15 grams
Saturated Fat . . . . 0 grams	Sodium . . . . 233 milligrams
Calories from fat 11	w/o bacon bits . . . . . 218 milligrams
Cholesterol . . . . 33 milligrams	

SPICY TURKEY CHILI

6 servings/serving size: 1 cup

This chili tastes great with fresh-baked Corn Muffins (see recipe, page 32).

- **2 onions, chopped**
- **2 garlic cloves, minced**
- **1/2 cup chopped green pepper**
- **1 Tbsp. olive oil**
- **1 lb. lean ground turkey breast meat** (the meat department at the supermarket will grind this up for you)
- **2 cups kidney or pinto beans**
- **2 cups canned tomatoes with liquid**
- **1 cup low-sodium chicken broth**
- **2 Tbsp. chili powder**
- **2 tsp. cumin**
- **Fresh ground pepper**

1. In a large saucepan, saute the onion, garlic, and green pepper in the oil for 10 minutes. Add the turkey meat and saute until turkey meat is cooked, about 5 to 10 minutes. Drain any fat away.
2. Add the remaining ingredients, bring to a boil, lower the heat and simmer uncovered for 30 minutes. Add additional chili powder if you like your chili extra spicy.

....

Lean Meat Exchange 2	Cholesterol . . . . 51 milligrams
Starch/Bread Exchange 1-1/2	Total Carbohydrate . . . . 23 grams
Calories 220	Dietary Fiber . . . . 5 grams
Total Fat . . . . 4 grams	Sugars . . . . 5 grams
Saturated Fat . . . . 1 gram	Protein . . . . 25 grams
Calories from fat 32	Sodium . . . . 175 milligrams

PASTA FAGIOLI

12 servings/serving size: 3/4–1 cup

*T*his hearty Italian soup freezes well, so you'll get several meals out of this recipe.

- 1 Tbsp. olive oil
- 1 large onion, chopped
- 3 cloves garlic, crushed
- 2 medium carrots, sliced
- 2 medium zucchini, sliced
- 2 tsp. basil
- 2 tsp. oregano

- 32 oz. unsalted tomatoes with liquid
- 32 ounces white cannelini or navy beans, drained and rinsed
- 1 lb. uncooked rigatoni or shell macaroni

1. Heat the oil in a large saucepan and saute the onions and garlic for 5 minutes.
2. Add the carrots, zucchini, basil, oregano, tomatoes with their liquid, and the beans. Cook until the vegetables are tender, about 15 to 17 minutes.
3. Cook the pasta according to package directions (without adding salt). Add the pasta and mix thoroughly. Serve warm with crusty bread.

....

Starch/Bread Exchange	3	Cholesterol	0 milligrams
Vegetable Exchange	1	Total Carbohydrate	51 grams
Calories	263	Dietary Fiber	4 grams
Total Fat	2 grams	Sugars	10 grams
Saturated Fat	0 grams	Protein	11 grams
Calories from fat	19	Sodium	115 milligrams

TASTY VEGETABLE SOUPS

HEARTY VEGETABLE SOUP

8 servings/serving size: about 1 cup

- 1-1/2 quarts low-sodium chicken broth
- 28 oz. whole tomatoes, chopped and drained
- 1 cup chopped onion
- 1 cup diced potatoes
- 1 cup sliced carrots
- 1 cup yellow corn
- 1 cup frozen or fresh shelled peas
- 1 cup cooked kidney, black or pinto beans (drained and rinsed, if canned)
- 2 tsp. oregano
- 1 Tbsp. minced fresh parsley
- 1 bay leaf
- Fresh ground pepper

Combine all ingredients in a large saucepot. Bring to a boil. Reduce the heat and simmer 1 hour until vegetables are tender. Remove bay leaf before serving.

Starch/Bread Exchange 1-1/2	Cholesterol .... 1 milligram
Vegetable Exchange 1	Total Carbohydrate .... 26 grams
Calories 142	Dietary Fiber .... 6 grams
Total Fat .... 2 grams	Sugars .... 7 grams
Saturated Fat .... 0 grams	Protein .... 7 grams
Calories from fat 17	Sodium .... 314 milligrams

ITALIAN MINESTRONE

8 servings/serving size: 1 cup

*T*his soup is traditionally served with warm, crusty French bread.

- 1 Tbsp. olive oil
- 1/2 cup sliced onion
- 4 cups low-sodium chicken broth
- 3/4 cup sliced carrot
- 1/2 cup sliced potato (with peel)
- 2 cups sliced cabbage or coarsely chopped spinach
- 1 cup sliced zucchini
- 1/2 cup cooked garbanzo beans (drained and rinsed, if canned)

- 1/2 cup cooked navy beans (drained and rinsed, if canned)
- 16 oz. canned tomatoes, with liquid
- 1/2 cup sliced celery
- 2 tsp. dried basil
- 1 tsp. dried oregano
- 1/2 cup uncooked rotini or other shaped pasta
- 1 Tbsp. minced fresh parsley

1. In a large soup pot over medium heat, saute the onion in oil until onion is slightly browned. Add the chicken broth, carrot, and potatoes. Cover and cook over medium heat for 30 minutes.
2. Add remaining ingredients and cook for an additional 15 to 20 minutes until the pasta is cooked through.

....

Starch/Bread Exchange	1	Cholesterol	0 milligrams
Vegetable Exchange	1	Total Carbohydrate	19 grams
Calories	116	Dietary Fiber	4 grams
Total Fat	3 grams	Sugars	5 grams
Saturated Fat	0 grams	Protein	5 grams
Calories from fat	25	Sodium	188 milligrams

LENTIL SOUP

8 servings/serving size: 1 cup

*C*ooking with lentils is a tasty and inexpensive way to include high-quality protein and complex carbohydrates in your diet—and they're easy to use because they don't require presoaking! This is a thick, hearty soup.

- 1 large onion, diced
- 1 large carrot, peeled and diced
- 2 stalks celery, diced
- 2 Tbsp. olive oil
- 1 lb. lentils
- 1-1/2 quarts low-sodium chicken or beef broth
- 2 medium russet or white potatoes, peeled and diced
- 1 tsp. oregano
- 1 tsp. thyme
- Fresh ground pepper

1. In a stockpot or Dutch oven, saute the onion, carrot, and celery in the olive oil for 10 minutes. Add the lentils, broth, and potatoes.
2. Continue to cook for 30 to 45 minutes, adding the oregano and thyme 15 minutes prior to serving time. Soup will keep 3 days in the refrigerator or can be frozen for 3 months.

....

Starch/Bread Exchange 3	Cholesterol .... 1 milligram
Fat Exchange 1/2	Total Carbohydrate .... 42 grams
Calories 275	Dietary Fiber .... 13 grams
Total Fat .... 5 grams	Sugars .... 7 grams
Saturated Fat .... 1 gram	Protein .... 16 grams
Calories from fat 48	Sodium .... 75 milligrams

HOW TO MAKE GREAT STOCKS

Here are some hints to help you make better soup stocks!

◆ Resist the temptation to throw all the leftovers from the week before into the pot. You need to start with good, fresh ingredients—and good doesn't have to mean expensive. For chicken stock all you really need is wings, backs, a few onions, carrots, celery, and a sprig or two of parsley.

◆ Vegetables should be scrubbed well, but can be left unpeeled. Onion skins give the stock a rich color. Avoid using cruciferous vegetables such as broccoli or cabbage—they produce an unpleasant taste when they are cooked for a long period of time.

◆ Always start cooking your stock with cold water. As you cook the stock, the water slowly heats until the vegetables are gently simmering. It is this period of long simmering that extracts the flavors of the stock ingredients. If you don't have tasty water in your area, use bottled spring water.

◆ Stock can be stored in the refrigerator for up to three days. It may also be frozen and placed in quart-size containers or in ice cube trays. Frozen stocks can be stored up to three months.

VEGETABLE STOCK

6 servings/serving size: 1 cup

Remember to include the onion skins to give this stock its rich color!

- 1 Tbsp. olive oil
- 2 carrots, coarsely chopped
- 2 celery stalks, coarsely chopped
- 1 large yellow onion, unpeeled, coarsely chopped
- 1 leek, sliced, white part only
- 1-1/2 quarts cold water
- 1 medium russet or white potato
- 3 parsley sprigs
- 1 fresh thyme sprig
- 3 black peppercorns

1. Heat the oil in a stockpot over medium heat. Add the carrots, celery, onion, and leek. Cook, stirring, for 4 minutes.
2. Reduce the heat to low, partially cover the pot, and cook the vegetables for 10 minutes until soft. Add the remaining ingredients and bring the stock to boil.
3. Reduce the heat to a simmer and cook, with pot partially covered, for 2 to 3 hours. Strain the stock and pour into a container. Cover and refrigerate or freeze.

....

Fat Exchange	1/2	Total Carbohydrate	1 gram
Calories	24	Dietary Fiber	0 grams
Total Fat	2 grams	Sugars	0 grams
Saturated Fat	0 grams	Protein	0 grams
Calories from fat	20	Sodium	0 milligrams
Cholesterol	0 milligrams		

CHICKEN STOCK

10 servings/serving size: 1 cup

You can use almost any chicken part in this recipe—handy if you like to buy whole chickens.

- 3 lb. chicken parts, washed
- 2 medium carrots, peeled and cut into chunks
- 2 parsley sprigs
- 1 tsp. dried basil
- 3 medium onions, unpeeled, quartered
- 3 garlic cloves, chopped
- 2 bay leaves
- 1/4 tsp. peppercorns
- 3 quarts water

1. In a large stockpot over medium heat, combine all ingredients. Bring to a boil, partially cover, and simmer for 5 to 6 hours.
2. Remove from heat and allow the stock to come to room temperature. Refrigerate stock overnight and remove fat layer when hardened.
3. Warm stock and strain. Store stock in refrigerator or freezer until ready to use.

....

* Free Food

Calories 13

Total Fat . . . . 0 grams

    Saturated Fat . . . . 0 grams

    Calories from fat 3

Cholesterol . . . . 1 milligram

Total Carbohydrate . . . . 2 grams

    Dietary Fiber . . . . 0 grams

    Sugars . . . . 2 grams

Protein . . . . 1 gram

Sodium . . . . 5 milligrams

* Remember that only 1 cup or less is a Free Food!

BEEF STOCK

10 servings/serving size: 1 cup

Y*our stock will have more flavor if you use beef bones with some meat on them.*

- ◆ 4 lb. beef bones
- ◆ 3 large onions, unpeeled, quartered
- ◆ 2 medium carrots, peeled and sliced
- ◆ 2 large garlic cloves
- ◆ 1 tsp. celery seeds
- ◆ 1-1/2 cups low-sodium tomato juice
- ◆ 1 tsp. dried thyme
- ◆ 1 tsp. dried marjoram
- ◆ 2 large bay leaves
- ◆ 4 parsley sprigs
- ◆ 1/4 tsp. peppercorns
- ◆ Water

1. Brown the bones in a roasting pan at 400 degrees for 25 to 30 minutes. Add onions, carrots, and garlic. Continue browning for 30 minutes, or until bones are well-browned.
2. Transfer to a large stockpot and add remaining ingredients. Add enough cold water to cover ingredients by 1 inch. Bring to a boil, reduce heat and let simmer for 5 to 10 minutes, removing any sediment that forms on top. Let simmer for 4 to 8 hours, partially covered.
3. When stock is finished cooking, bring to room temperature before refrigerating. Refrigerate uncovered overnight. Remove surface fat. Strain the stock and taste; if flavor is weak, continue to cook, allowing more liquid to evaporate. Store stock in freezer until ready to use.

....

* Free Food

Calories 19

Total Fat . . . . 0 grams

   Saturated Fat . . . . 0 grams

   Calories from fat 3

Cholesterol . . . . 1 milligram

Total Carbohydrate . . . . 3 grams

   Dietary Fiber . . . . 0 grams

   Sugars . . . . 3 grams

Protein . . . . 1 gram

Sodium . . . . 9 milligrams

* Remember that only 1 cup or less is a Free Food!

MUSHROOM AND BARLEY SOUP

6 servings/serving size: 1 cup

Barley adds fiber and a rich flavor to soup.

- 1/2 cup barley
- 6 cups water
- 1 large carrot, diced
- 2 cups diced celery
- 2 bay leaves
- 1/4 cup minced fresh parsley
- 1 tsp. dried thyme

- 1 medium onion, diced
- 2 Tbsp. olive oil
- 1/2 lb. mushrooms, sliced
- 1 garlic clove, minced
- 2 Tbsp. lite soy sauce
- 2 Tbsp. fresh lemon juice
- Fresh ground pepper

1. Place barley and water in a 2-quart saucepan; bring to a boil. Reduce heat and let simmer; add carrot, celery, bay leaves, parsley, and thyme.
2. Return to a boil, reduce the heat, cover, and let simmer 1 hour. When the barley has been cooking about 45 minutes, use a small skillet to saute the onion in the olive oil for about 5 minutes.
3. Add the mushrooms and saute until tender. Add the mushroom mixture to the barley, along with the remaining ingredients. Continue to simmer for 10 more minutes.

....

Starch/Bread Exchange 1-1/2	Cholesterol .... 0 milligrams
Fat Exchange 1/2	Total Carbohydrate .... 22 grams
Calories 140	Dietary Fiber .... 5 grams
Total Fat .... 5 grams	Sugars .... 5 grams
Saturated Fat .... 1 gram	Protein .... 3 grams
Calories from fat 45	Sodium .... 262 milligrams

MUSHROOM AND SHERRY BISQUE*

3 servings/serving size: 1 cup

*T*he sherry gives the mushrooms in this bisque a special flavor!

- 1/2 lb. fresh mushrooms, finely chopped (chop a few coarsely)
- 1 small onion, quartered, finely chopped
- 2 cups low-sodium chicken broth
- 2 Tbsp. dry sherry
- 1-1/2 Tbsp. canola oil
- 2 Tbsp. flour
- 1/2 cup skim milk
- 1-1/2 cups half-and-half
- Dash salt and pepper

1. In a medium saucepan, combine the mushrooms, onion, chicken broth, and sherry. Cover and let simmer for 10 to 15 minutes, stirring occasionally.
2. In a separate medium saucepan over medium-low heat, heat the oil. Add the flour and mix well. Add the milk and half-and-half; continue cooking until thickened, stirring constantly.
3. Stir in mushroom mixture and season with salt and pepper to serve.

....

Fat Exchange	4	Cholesterol	46 milligrams
Starch/Bread Exchange	1-1/2	Total Carbohydrate	17 grams
Calories	303	Dietary Fiber	2 grams
Total Fat	22 grams	Sugars	10 grams
Saturated Fat	10 grams	Protein	8 grams
Calories from fat	201	Sodium	152 milligrams

* This dish is relatively high in fat!

CREAM OF CARROT SOUP

4 servings/serving size: 1 cup

This smooth, tasty soup is great to serve for special luncheons.

- ◆ 2 Tbsp. low-sodium chicken broth
- ◆ 3 Tbsp. finely chopped shallots or onions
- ◆ 2 Tbsp. flour
- ◆ 1 cup skim milk, scalded and hot

- ◆ 1 tsp. cinnamon
- ◆ 1 cup cooked, pureed carrots
- ◆ 1 cup low-sodium chicken broth
- ◆ Fresh ground pepper

1. Heat the broth in a stockpot over medium heat. Add shallots and cook until they are limp. Sprinkle shallots with flour and cook 2 to 3 minutes.
2. Pour in the hot milk and cook until mixture thickens. Add remaining ingredients. Bring almost to a boil, stirring often. Add pepper to taste.

Starch/Bread Exchange 1
Calories 74
Total Fat . . . . 1 gram
   Saturated Fat . . . . 0 grams
   Calories from fat 6
Cholesterol . . . . 1 milligram

Total Carbohydrate . . . . 13 grams
   Dietary Fiber . . . . 2 grams
   Sugars . . . . 6 grams
Protein . . . . 4 grams
Sodium . . . . 86 milligrams

FRENCH ONION SOUP

4 servings/serving size: 1 cup

This version of a very popular soup is altered slightly—the fat content is much lower, yet the authentic taste is all here!

- ◆ 1 lb. yellow onions, thinly sliced
- ◆ 2 Tbsp. olive oil
- ◆ 1 tsp. brown sugar substitute
- ◆ Fresh ground pepper
- ◆ Dash salt
- ◆ 1 Tbsp. unbleached flour

- ◆ 1 quart low-sodium beef broth
- ◆ 1/3 cup vermouth
- ◆ 4 slices French bread, toasted (about 3/4-inch slices)
- ◆ 1 cup shredded reduced-fat Swiss cheese

1. In a large saucepot, saute the onion in the oil for 15 minutes. Add the sugar, pepper, and salt. Simmer uncovered for 35 minutes, stirring occasionally, adding a little water if necessary. The onions will get very brown.

2. Add the flour and cook an additional 1 minute. Gradually add the beef broth and vermouth; cook over medium heat, stirring constantly until thickened and bubbly. Reduce the heat and simmer for 20 minutes.

3. Ladle the soup into 4 individual oven-proof soup bowls. Top each bowl with a slice of bread and some cheese. Place under the broiler for 2 to 3 minutes. Carefully remove from the oven and serve.

Starch/Bread Exchange 2	Cholesterol . . . . 22 milligrams
Fat Exchange 2	Total Carbohydrate . . . . 27 grams
Lean Meat Exchange 1	Dietary Fiber . . . . 2 grams
Calories 307	Sugars . . . . 10 grams
Total Fat . . . . 15 grams	Protein . . . . 14 grams
Saturated Fat . . . . 6 grams	Sodium . . . . 261 milligrams
Calories from fat 139	

WHITE BEAN SOUP

6 servings/serving size: 1 cup

Use any variety of white bean for this spectacular soup.

- 1/4 cup chopped onion
- 1 garlic clove, minced
- 2 Tbsp. olive oil
- 1/2 lb. dried great northern beans, white navy beans or canellini beans
- 2 quarts water
- 2 bay leaves
- 1 tsp. dried basil
- Dash salt and pepper
- 2 medium scallions, chopped
- 2 Tbsp. minced fresh parsley

1. In a large saucepan, saute the onion and garlic in the oil for 5 minutes. Add the beans, water, bay leaves, and basil; stir well. Bring mixture to a boil, reduce the heat, cover and let simmer.
2. Continue to cook the soup for 2 hours or until beans are tender. Add water (if necessary), salt and pepper; mix well.
3. In a blender or food processor, puree the mixture. Return the soup back to the saucepan and serve hot. Garnish with scallions and parsley.

....

Starch/Bread Exchange 1-1/2	Cholesterol . . . . 0 milligrams
Fat Exchange 1/2	Total Carbohydrate . . . . 22 grams
Calories 157	Dietary Fiber . . . . 6 grams
Total Fat . . . . 5 grams	Sugars . . . . 2 grams
Saturated Fat . . . . 1 gram	Protein . . . . 8 grams
Calories from fat 43	Sodium . . . . 28 milligrams

SPANISH BLACK BEAN SOUP

6 servings/serving size: 1 cup

The combination of red wine and black beans gives this soup its robust flavor.

- 2 tsp. chicken broth
- 1 tsp. olive oil
- 3 garlic cloves, minced
- 1 yellow onion, minced
- 1 tsp. minced fresh oregano
- 1 tsp. cumin
- 1 tsp. chili powder or 1/2 tsp. cayenne pepper

- 1 red pepper, chopped
- 1 carrot, coarsely chopped
- 3 cups cooked black beans
- 1-1/2 cups low-sodium chicken broth
- 1/2 cup dry red wine

1. In a large stockpot, heat 2 tsp. chicken broth, and olive oil. Add garlic and onions and saute for 3 minutes. Add oregano, cumin, and chili powder; stir for another minute. Add the red pepper and carrot.

2. Puree 1-1/2 cups of the black beans in a blender or food processor. Add the pureed beans, remaining 1-1/2 cups whole black beans, chicken broth, and red wine to the stockpot. Simmer 1 hour. Taste before serving; add additional spices if you like.

....

Starch/Bread Exchange 2	Total Carbohydrate .... 26 grams	
Calories 155	Dietary Fiber .... 6 grams	
Total Fat .... 2 grams	Sugars .... 6 grams	
Saturated Fat .... 0 grams	Protein .... 9 grams	
Calories from fat 15	Sodium .... 29 milligrams	
Cholesterol .... 0 milligrams		

MEXICAN TORTILLA SOUP

8 servings/serving size: 1 cup

*S*trips of tortillas lace this spicy, hearty soup.

- 2 tsp. olive oil
- 1 onion, chopped
- 2 cloves garlic, minced
- 1 Tbsp. chopped fresh cilantro
- 1 Tbsp. cumin
- 1 tsp. cayenne pepper
- 1 quart low-sodium chicken broth
- 1 15-oz. can whole tomatoes, drained and coarsely chopped
- 1 medium zucchini, sliced
- 1 medium yellow squash, sliced
- 1 cup yellow corn
- 6 corn tortillas
- 8 Tbsp. shredded low-fat cheese (optional)

1. In a large saucepan, saute the onion and garlic in the oil for 5 minutes.
2. Add the cilantro, cumin, and cayenne pepper; saute for 3 more minutes. Add remaining ingredients except the tortillas and optional cheese. Bring to a boil; cover and let simmer for 30 minutes.
3. Cut each tortilla into about 10 strips. Place the strips on a cookie sheet and bake for 5–6 minutes at 350 degrees until slightly browned and toasted. Remove from the oven.
4. To serve the soup, place strips of tortilla into each bowl. Ladle the soup on top of the tortilla strips. Top with cheese if desired.

....

* Starch/Bread Exchange 1	Cholesterol . . . . 1 milligram (6)
Vegetable Exchange 1	Total Carbohydrate . . . 20 grams (21)
(Fat Exchange) . . . . (1/2)	Dietary Fiber . . . . 4 grams (4)
Calories 113 (133)	Sugars . . . . 5 grams (5)
Total Fat . . . . 3 grams (4)	Protein . . . . 4 grams (6)
Saturated Fat . . . . 1 gram (1)	Sodium . . . . 190 milligrams (243)
Calories from fat 24 (36)	

* Values in parentheses indicate use of optional cheese!

GAZPACHO*

4 servings/serving size: 1-1/2 cups

*S*erve this cool, refreshing vegetable and tomato broth on hot summer days.

- 1 garlic clove, crushed
- 1 Tbsp. olive oil
- 1 large onion, chopped
- 5 medium peeled tomatoes
- 1 cup low-sodium chicken broth
- 2 Tbsp. red wine vinegar
- 1 tsp. hot pepper sauce (Tabasco)

- 1/4 tsp. paprika
- 1 large green or red pepper, chopped
- 1 cup peeled, seeded and chopped cucumber
- 1/4 cup chopped scallions

1. Combine the garlic, oil, onion, and tomatoes in a food processor and process until smooth. Add the broth, vinegar, and liquid hot pepper sauce; process again. Transfer the mixture to a large soup tureen or bowl.
2. Add the red or green pepper, cucumber, and scallions. Chill in the refrigerator overnight. Serve the soup in bowls or large wine glasses. Top with croutons if desired.

....

Starch/Bread Exchange	1	Cholesterol	1 milligram
Vegetable Exchange	1	Total Carbohydrate	20 grams
Fat Exchange	1/2	Dietary Fiber	5 grams
Calories	136	Sugars	14 grams
Total Fat	5 grams	Protein	6 grams
Saturated Fat	1 gram	Sodium	412 milligrams
Calories from fat	44		

* This soup is relatively high in sodium!

WARM BREADS & MUFFINS

BUTTERMILK BISCUITS

12 servings/serving size: 1 biscuit

- **2 cups whole wheat pastry flour or unbleached white flour**
- **1 Tbsp. baking powder**
- **1/2 tsp. baking soda**
- **1 cup low-fat buttermilk**
- **3 Tbsp. canola oil**

1. Preheat the oven to 425 degrees. Lightly spray two cookie sheets with nonstick cooking spray.
2. In a medium bowl, combine the flour, baking powder, and baking soda. Add the buttermilk and oil; mix with a fork until well-blended.
3. Drop the dough by heaping tablespoons onto cookie sheets, 1-1/2 inches apart. Bake for 10 to 12 minutes until lightly browned.

··

Starch/Bread Exchange	1	Cholesterol	1 milligram
Fat Exchange	1/2	Total Carbohydrate	17 grams
Calories	116	Dietary Fiber	1 gram
Total Fat	4 grams	Sugars	1 gram
Saturated Fat	0 grams	Protein	3 grams
Calories from fat	35	Sodium	134 milligrams

SPOON BREAD

16 servings/serving size: 1/2 cup

Old-fashioned spoon bread is great with any meal!

- ◆ 2 cups water
- ◆ 2 cups yellow cornmeal
- ◆ 2 tsp. baking powder
- ◆ 1-1/2 tsp. baking soda

- ◆ 1 tsp. salt (optional)
- ◆ 2 cups skim milk
- ◆ 2 egg substitute equivalents

1. In a bowl, combine 1 cup of the water with the cornmeal, baking powder, salt and baking soda.
2. In a 3-quart saucepan, heat the remaining 1 cup water to boiling; reduce the heat to low and stir in the cornmeal mixture. Cook the mixture until thick and remove from heat.
3. Preheat the oven to 350 degrees. Lightly spray a 2-quart casserole dish with nonstick cooking spray. First add the milk, then the eggs, into the cornmeal mixture and beat until smooth. Pour into the casserole dish. Bake 1 hour until set; serve warm.

....

Starch/Bread Exchange 1		Total Carbohydrate . . . . 15 grams		
Calories 79		Dietary Fiber . . . . 1 gram		
Total Fat . . . . 0 grams		Sugars . . . . 1 gram		
Saturated Fat . . . . 0 grams		Protein . . . . 3 grams		
Calories from fat 3		Sodium . . . . 276 milligrams		
Cholesterol . . . . 1 milligram		w/o added salt . . . . . 142 milligrams		

IRISH SODA BREAD

10 servings/serving size: one 1-inch slice

There is nothing like warm Irish Soda Bread!

- 2 cups unbleached white flour
- 1 tsp. baking soda
- 2 Tbsp. low-calorie margarine, chilled and cut into bits
- 1 Tbsp. caraway seeds
- 1/4 cup dried currants or raisins
- 1 cup low-fat buttermilk

1. Preheat the oven to 375 degrees. Combine the flour and baking soda. With 2 knives or a pastry blender, work in the margarine until the mixture resembles coarse crumbs.

2. Toss in the caraway seeds and currants. With a fork, mix in the buttermilk and mix until just blended. Turn the dough out onto a lightly floured surface and knead very gently for 20 strokes, just until smooth. Do not overwork the dough.

3. Pat well into a 9-inch pan or shape well on a baking sheet. Make a shallow 4-inch cross in the center of the loaf and bake for 25 to 30 minutes until golden. Serve warm.

....

Starch/Bread Exchange	1-1/2	Total Carbohydrate	23 grams
Calories	122	Dietary Fiber	1 gram
Total Fat	2 grams	Sugars	4 grams
Saturated Fat	0 grams	Protein	4 grams
Calories from fat	14	Sodium	127 milligrams
Cholesterol	1 milligram		

CORN MUFFINS

12 servings/serving size: 1 muffin

Use some of the variations included below to create interesting corn muffins. (The variations do not significantly alter the nutrient exchange information.)

- ◆ 1 cup yellow cornmeal
- ◆ 1/2 tsp. baking soda
- ◆ 1/2 tsp. baking powder
- ◆ 1/4 tsp. salt (optional)

- ◆ 1 cup low-fat buttermilk
- ◆ 1 egg substitute equivalent
- ◆ 1 Tbsp. canola oil

1. Preheat the oven to 425 degrees. Combine the cornmeal, baking soda, baking powder and salt; mix thoroughly. Stir in buttermilk, egg and oil; blend well.
2. Coat muffin pans with nonstick cooking spray. Spoon batter into muffin pans, filling the cups 2/3 full. Bake for 10 to 12 minutes or until tops are golden brown. Serve warm.

Variations: add 1/2 cup cooked corn kernels, 1/2 cup finely diced green or red pepper, or 1/2 cup finely diced sauteed onions to the batter.

....

Starch/Bread Exchange 1
Calories 164
Total Fat .... 2 grams
   Saturated Fat .... 0 grams
   Calories from fat 14
Cholesterol .... 1 milligram

Total Carbohydrate .... 10 grams
   Dietary Fiber .... 1 gram
   Sugars .... 1 gram
Protein .... 2 grams
Sodium .... 120 milligrams
   w/o added salt ...... 76 milligrams

DATE NUT BREAD

16 servings/serving size: one 1-inch slice

This bread tastes great with fruit or chicken salads.

- 1-3/4 cups chopped, pitted dates
- 1-1/4 cups boiling water
- 2-1/4 cups whole wheat flour
- 1/2 cup chopped walnuts
- 1 tsp. baking soda
- 1 egg substitute equivalent
- 1/2 cup unsweetened applesauce
- 2 Tbsp. fructose
- 1 tsp. vanilla or almond extract

1. In a bowl, combine the dates and boiling water; let stand for 15 minutes. Lightly coat a 9x5-inch loaf pan with nonstick cooking spray. Preheat the oven to 350 degrees.
2. In a large bowl, combine the flour, nuts, and baking soda. Add the egg, applesauce, fructose and extract. Add the dates and mix well.
3. Pour mixture into the prepared pan and bake for 65 minutes or until a toothpick inserted in the center comes out clean. Cool in the pan on a rack for 10 minutes. Remove from the pan and serve warm or cold.

....

Starch/Bread Exchange 1	Cholesterol .... 0 milligrams
Fruit Exchange 1	Total Carbohydrate .... 28 grams
Calories 140	Dietary Fiber .... 4 grams
Total Fat .... 3 grams	Sugars .... 14 grams
Saturated Fat .... 0 grams	Protein .... 3 grams
Calories from fat 23	Sodium .... 58 milligrams

BANANA CARROT MUFFINS

12 servings/serving size: 1 muffin

These muffins are moist, sweet and full of good-for-you ingredients!

- 1-1/2 cups whole wheat or unbleached flour
- 2 tsp. baking powder
- 1 tsp. baking soda
- 1/2 tsp. nutmeg
- Pinch cloves
- 2 egg substitute equivalents
- 1/2 cup unsweetened applesauce
- 2 Tbsp. fructose
- 1/2 cup low-fat buttermilk
- 1/2 cup mashed banana
- 1 cup grated carrot
- 1 tsp. vanilla

1. Preheat the oven to 400 degrees. Combine the first 5 ingredients together in a large bowl. Combine the remaining ingredients in a smaller bowl. Combine all ingredients together and mix well, but do not over-beat.
2. Spoon into muffin cups and bake for 20 minutes. Serve warm or at room temperature.

....

Starch/Bread Exchange 1	Total Carbohydrate .... 18 grams
Calories 88	Dietary Fiber .... 1 gram
Total Fat .... 0 grams	Sugars .... 5 grams
Saturated Fat .... 0 grams	Protein .... 3 gram
Calories from fat 3	Sodium .... 149 milligrams
Cholesterol .... 0 milligrams	

SWEET POTATO AND ZUCCHINI BREAD

16 servings/serving size: one 1-inch slice

This fiber-rich, slightly spicy bread is especially good around holiday time.

- 2 cups whole wheat or unbleached flour
- 1 tsp. baking powder
- 1/2 tsp. baking soda
- 2 tsp. cinnamon
- 3 egg substitute equivalents
- 3/4 cup unsweetened applesauce
- 1/4 cup fructose
- 1 tsp. vanilla extract
- 1-1/2 cups grated zucchini, unpeeled
- 1-1/2 cups grated raw sweet potato, peeled

1. Preheat the oven to 350 degrees. Spray a 9x5x3-inch loaf pan with nonstick cooking spray and set aside.
2. Combine the first four ingredients in a medium bowl. In a larger bowl, beat together the eggs, applesauce, fructose, and vanilla. Mix in the zucchini and sweet potatoes. Add the flour mixture to the bowl and mix well.
3. Transfer the batter to the prepared pan; bake for 1 hour and 15 minutes. Cool bread in the pan for 15 minutes. Turn bread onto a rack and cool completely. Slice and serve.

....

Starch/Bread Exchange	1	Total Carbohydrate	19 grams
Calories	89	Dietary Fiber	1 gram
Total Fat	0 grams	Sugars	6 grams
Saturated Fat	0 grams	Protein	3 grams
Calories from fat	2	Sodium	68 milligrams
Cholesterol	0 milligrams		

CRANBERRY ORANGE SCONES

8 servings/serving size: 1 scone

These scones—low-fat and homemade—are wonderful with soup or salad.

- 1/2 cup dried cranberries
- 2 Tbsp. fructose
- 1/2 cup low-fat buttermilk, room temperature
- 3/4 cup fresh orange juice
- Grated peel of one large orange
- 2-1/4 cups whole wheat pastry flour or unbleached flour
- 1 tsp. baking soda
- 1 tsp. cream of tartar
- 1/2 tsp. salt
- 2 Tbsp. low-calorie margarine, cold

1. Preheat the oven to 375 degrees. Sprinkle a cookie sheet with flour. Soak the dried cranberries in boiling water for 5 minutes. Drain and set aside. In a small bowl, mix together the fructose and buttermilk. Add orange juice and rind.
2. Sift flour, baking soda, cream of tartar and salt in a large bowl. Using a fork or fingers, cut in the margarine until well combined. Stir in the buttermilk mixture and cranberries into flour mixture and mix very gently by hand until combined.
3. Turn out the batter onto the floured cookie sheet and pat into a circle about 3/4-inch thick, 8 inches across. Using a sharp knife, cut the circle into 8 wedges.
4. Place the pan in the oven and bake for 25 minutes. Cool and cut completely through the wedge cuts to serve.

....

Starch/Bread Exchange 2-1/2	Total Carbohydrate .... 40 grams
Calories 195	Dietary Fiber .... 1 gram
Total Fat .... 2 grams	Sugars .... 13 grams
Saturated Fat .... 0 grams	Protein .... 5 grams
Calories from fat 18	Sodium .... 275 milligrams
Cholesterol .... 1 milligram	

SEAFOOD & PASTA SALADS

PASTA SALAD WITH BASIL VINAIGRETTE

8 servings/serving size: 1 cup

- 2 lb. fresh plum tomatoes, cut into 1/2-inch cubes
- 1/4 cup olive oil
- 1/4 cup chopped fresh basil leaves
- 2 Tbsp. balsamic vinegar
- Fresh ground pepper
- 1/2 cup chopped red onion
- 1/2 cup minced red bell pepper
- 1 lb. uncooked pasta

Prepare pasta according to package directions (without adding salt), drain and set aside. Combine tomatoes, oil, vinegar and pepper in a large bowl. Combine the red onion, red pepper and pasta together in a separate bowl. Add the tomato mixture to the pasta and toss well. Serve.

....

Starch/Bread Exchange 3	Cholesterol .... 0 milligrams
Vegetable Exchange 1	Total Carbohydrate .... 48 grams
Fat Exchange 1	Dietary Fiber .... 3 grams
Calories 297	Sugars .... 6 grams
Total Fat .... 8 grams	Protein .... 8 grams
Saturated Fat .... 1 gram	Sodium .... 14 milligrams
Calories from fat 73	

CALIFORNIA SEAFOOD SALAD

8 servings/serving size: 4 oz.

Try using pieces of crab or lobster instead of, or in addition to, the shrimp and scallops.

- 1/4 lb. fresh green beans, cut in 1-inch pieces
- 1 Tbsp. olive oil
- 1 lb. fresh scallops
- 1 lb. uncooked fresh shrimp, peeled and deveined
- 1/2 cup low-fat sour cream
- 2 Tbsp. low-fat mayonnaise
- 2 Tbsp. skim milk
- 1 Tbsp. chopped fresh dill
- 2 Tbsp. chopped fresh parsley
- 2 Tbsp. fresh lime juice
- 1 head romaine lettuce
- 1 large tomato, cut in wedges
- 1 lemon, cut into wedges

1. To prepare the salad, steam the green beans for 3 to 4 minutes until cooked, but slightly crunchy. Set aside. In a large skillet, heat the olive oil.
2. Add the scallops and shrimp and saute over medium heat for 4 to 5 minutes until the seafood is cooked (the shrimp turn pink and the scallops are no longer translucent). Set aside to cool while you prepare the dressing.
3. Combine all the dressing ingredients together in a small bowl. Add the dressing to the seafood and mix well. Add the green beans and toss again.
4. To assemble, place lettuce leaves on individual plates or one platter. Place seafood salad in a mound on top of the lettuce. Surround the salad with tomato and lemon wedges.

....

Lean Meat Exchange 2	Cholesterol . . . . 87 milligrams
Vegetable Exchange 1	Total Carbohydrate . . . . 7 grams
Calories 143	Dietary Fiber . . . . 2 grams
Total Fat . . . . 5 grams	Sugars . . . . 4 grams
Saturated Fat . . . . 1 gram	Protein . . . . 18 grams
Calories from fat 45	Sodium . . . . 226 milligrams

SHRIMP AND PASTA SALAD

8 servings/serving size: 1 cup

Shells, shrimp and a bit of Romano cheese make this salad tasty and festive.

- 1 lb. uncooked shell macaroni
- 12 oz. frozen baby shrimp
- 6 scallions, thinly sliced
- 3 small zucchini, sliced
- 10 cherry tomatoes, halved
- 1 Tbsp. dried Italian seasoning
- 1 Tbsp. minced fresh garlic
- Fresh ground pepper
- 1 Tbsp. grated Romano cheese
- 1/4 cup olive oil
- 1/3 cup red wine vinegar
- 1 small head butter lettuce

1. Cook the shell macaroni in boiling water for 6 to 7 minutes, adding the frozen shrimp after 4 minutes. Drain and let cool.
2. In a large bowl, combine the macaroni, shrimp, scallions, zucchini and tomatoes. Sprinkle with Italian seasoning, garlic, pepper and cheese and mix well.
3. Drizzle the olive oil and vinegar on top and toss until well coated; refrigerate until chilled. To serve, line a clear glass bowl with lettuce leaves and spoon mixture into the bowl.

....

Starch/Bread Exchange 3
Medium-Fat Meat Exchange 1
Calories 329
Total Fat . . . . 9 grams
  Saturated Fat . . . . 1 gram
  Calories from fat 77
Cholesterol . . . . 72 milligrams
Total Carbohydrate . . . . 47 grams
  Dietary Fiber . . . . 3 grams
  Sugars . . . . 5 grams
Protein . . . . 16 grams
Sodium . . . . 105 milligrams

SHRIMP AND RADICCHIO SALAD

4 servings/serving size: about 1/3 cup

Radicchio is a very beautiful lettuce—its burgundy color adds eye appeal to any salad!

- 1/4 cup olive oil
- 2 Tbsp. red wine vinegar
- 3 medium garlic cloves, minced
- 1 medium shallot, minced
- 2 tsp. Dijon mustard
- 1 tsp. prepared horseradish

- Fresh ground pepper
- 1/2 pound cooked bay shrimp
- 1 medium head Boston lettuce, shredded
- 1 medium head radicchio lettuce, shredded

1. In a medium bowl, combine all the dressing ingredients. Add the shrimp and toss well. Refrigerate for 30 minutes.
2. Just before serving, combine lettuce and radicchio in a serving bowl. Place shrimp mixture on top, toss and serve.

....

Lean Meat Exchange 2
Vegetable Exchange 1
Fat Exchange 1-1/2
Calories 202
Total Fat . . . . 14 grams
   Saturated Fat . . . . 2 grams
   Calories from fat 130

Cholesterol . . . . 111 milligrams
Total Carbohydrate . . . . 5 grams
   Dietary Fiber . . . . 2 grams
   Sugars . . . . 2 grams
Protein . . . . 14 grams
Sodium . . . . 186 milligrams

FRESH SEAFOOD PASTA SALAD

12 servings/serving size: 3/4 cup

*T*his is a delicious medley of fresh fish, pasta and vegetables.

- 1 lb. cooked small pasta shells
- 2 medium carrots, peeled and diced
- 3/4 cup broccoli florets
- 1/2 medium red onion, diced
- 4 Tbsp. chopped cilantro
- 1 each red, yellow and green pepper, julienned
- 8 large cherry tomatoes, halved
- 4 medium celery stalks, diced
- 4 scallions, chopped
- 2 Tbsp. minced garlic
- 12 large pitted black olives
- 1/2 lb. cooked sea scallops
- 22 oz. uncooked fresh shrimp, peeled and deveined
- 1/2 lb. precooked crab legs
- 1/2 cup olive oil
- 1/3 cup red wine vinegar
- Fresh ground pepper

1. Blanch broccoli florets by placing in boiling water. Turn off the heat, wait 1 minute and drain the broccoli. Pour cool water over the broccoli to stop the cooking process and drain again.
2. Boil the shrimp until it just turns pink. Combine the pasta and vegetables in a large salad bowl. Add the cooked seafood and toss with the pasta and vegetables.
3. Combine the oil, vinegar and pepper. Pour dressing over salad and refrigerate for several hours before serving.

....

Medium-Fat Meat Exchange	1	Calories from fat	97
Starch/Bread Exchange	1	Cholesterol	90 milligrams
Vegetable Exchange	1	Total Carbohydrate	17 grams
Fat Exchange	1	Dietary Fiber	2 grams
Calories	226	Sugars	5 grams
Total Fat	11 grams	Protein	16 grams
Saturated Fat	2 grams	Sodium	242 milligrams

CRAB AND RICE SALAD

4 servings/serving size: 1/4 recipe

*B*rown rice gives this salad a great nutty taste.

- 1 cup uncooked brown rice
- 5 oz. fresh steamed crab meat, flaked
- 1 large tomato, diced
- 1/4 cup chopped green pepper
- 3 Tbsp. chopped fresh parsley
- 2 Tbsp. red onion

- 1/2 cup plain nonfat yogurt
- 1-1/2 Tbsp. lemon juice
- 1/4 tsp. salt (optional)
- Fresh ground pepper
- 1 head butter lettuce
- 1 large tomato, cut in wedges

1. In a medium saucepot, boil 2-1/2 cups of water. Slowly add 1 cup uncooked brown rice. Cover and lower the heat to low. Cook the rice for 45 to 50 minutes until tender. Do not continually stir the rice (this will cause it to become gummy). Just check occasionally.
2. In a large salad bowl, combine all the ingredients except the lettuce and tomato wedges. Just before serving, line plates with the lettuce and spoon salad on top of the lettuce. Garnish with tomato wedges.

Starch/Bread Exchange 2	Total Carbohydrate . . . . 31 grams
Vegetable Exchange 1	Dietary Fiber . . . . 4 grams
Calories 190	Sugars . . . . 6 grams
Total Fat . . . . 2 grams	Protein . . . . 13 grams
Saturated Fat . . . . 0 grams	Sodium . . . . 273 milligrams
Calories from fat 18	w/o added salt . . . . . 139 milligrams
Cholesterol . . . . 37 milligrams	

LOBSTER SALAD

6 servings/serving size: 1/2 cup

Lobster is a special treat your guests will appreciate!

- 2 lb. lobster in the shell or 1 lb. lobster meat
- 3/4 lb. small red potatoes
- 1/2 cup low-fat mayonnaise
- 3 Tbsp. plain low-fat yogurt
- 1 Tbsp. chopped fresh tarragon
- 1/4 cup chopped scallions
- Fresh ground pepper
- 1 small head romaine lettuce, washed and leaves separated

1. To prepare lobster in the shell, place the lobster in boiling water and boil until meat is tender, about 20 minutes. Cool the lobster, remove meat from the shell and cut into 1-inch cubes. You may also purchase lobster meat from the seafood department at the supermarket.
2. Wash, but do not peel the potatoes. Boil the potatoes in water until tender, about 15 to 20 minutes. Drain, cool and quarter. In a bowl, combine the remaining dressing ingredients. In a separate bowl, combine the lobster and potatoes.
3. Add dressing to the lobster and potatoes and mix well. To serve, line plates with lettuce. Spoon lobster salad over the lettuce.

. . . .

Lean Meat Exchange	2	Cholesterol	63 milligrams
Starch/Bread Exchange	1	Total Carbohydrate	15 grams
Calories	193	Dietary Fiber	2 grams
Total Fat	7 grams	Sugars	2 grams
Saturated Fat	1 gram	Protein	18 grams
Calories from fat	61	Sodium	417 milligrams

TORTELLINI AND FETA CHEESE SALAD*

6 servings/serving size: 1/2 cup

A little bit of this salad goes a long way—it's packed with tortellini, walnuts and feta cheese!

- 1/4 cup olive oil
- 1/4 cup white wine vinegar
- 1/4 cup sliced scallions
- 3 garlic cloves, minced
- 1 Tbsp. dried basil
- 1 tsp. dried dill
- 24 oz. frozen tortellini, stuffed with cheese
- 8 oz. water-packed artichoke hearts, drained and quartered
- 1/3 cup crumbled feta cheese
- 1/4 cup chopped black olives
- 1/4 cup chopped walnuts
- 1 large tomato, quartered

1. In a small bowl, whisk together the oil and vinegar. Add scallions, cloves, basil and dill; mix well.
2. Combine all the salad ingredients together and pour the dressing on top. Refrigerate overnight or at least 2 to 3 hours. Serve.

....

Fat Exchange	3	Cholesterol	51 milligrams
Starch/Bread Exchange	3	Total Carbohydrate	45 grams
Lean Meat Exchange	1	Dietary Fiber	3 grams
Calories	420	Sugars	5 grams
Total Fat	22 grams	Protein	14 grams
Saturated Fat	6 grams	Sodium	537 milligrams
Calories from fat	198		

* This recipe is relatively high in sodium and fat!

PASTA-STUFFED TOMATO SALAD

4 servings/serving size: 2/3 cup stuffing in 1 medium tomato

*T*his is a lovely salad to serve for a light luncheon.

- 1 cup uncooked corkscrew macaroni
- 2 small carrots, sliced
- 2 scallions, chopped
- 2 oz. pimentos, drained
- 1 cup cooked kidney beans
- 1/2 cup sliced celery
- 1/4 cup cooked peas
- 2 Tbsp. chopped fresh parsley
- 1/4 cup low-calorie Italian salad dressing
- 2 Tbsp. low-fat mayonnaise
- 1/4 tsp. dried marjoram
- Fresh ground pepper
- 4 medium tomatoes

1. Cook the corkscrew macaroni in boiling water until cooked, about 7 to 8 minutes; drain. In a large mixing bowl, combine the macaroni with the remaining salad ingredients and toss well. Cover and chill 1 hour or more.
2. With the stem end down, cut each tomato into 6 wedges, cutting to, but not through, the base of the tomato. Spread wedges slightly apart; spoon pasta mixture into tomatoes. Chill until ready to serve.

....

Starch/Bread Exchange	2	Cholesterol	3 milligrams
Vegetable Exchange	1	Total Carbohydrate	37 grams
Fat Exchange	1/2	Dietary Fiber	7 grams
Calories	207	Sugars	9 grams
Total Fat	4 grams	Protein	8 grams
Saturated Fat	1 gram	Sodium	303 milligrams
Calories from fat	34		

TUNA AND VEGETABLE SALAD

4 servings/serving size: 1 cup

*T*his very filling salad can be a one-bowl meal, especially if you add
some crusty rolls!

- ◆ 7 oz. water-packed tuna, drained
- ◆ 1 16-oz. can canellini beans, drained and rinsed
- ◆ 1 large red pepper, chopped
- ◆ 1/2 cup chopped fresh parsley
- ◆ 1/3 cup minced green onion

- ◆ 1/4 cup minced shallots
- ◆ 3 Tbsp. white wine vinegar
- ◆ 1 Tbsp. olive oil
- ◆ 1 Tbsp. dry white wine
- ◆ 1 tsp. cumin seeds
- ◆ Fresh ground pepper

Combine the tuna, beans, pepper, parsley, green onion and shallots.
Combine all the dressing ingredients and pour over the tuna mixture.
Refrigerate the salad for at least 1 hour and serve.

....

Lean Meat Exchange	2	Cholesterol	19 milligrams
Starch/Bread Exchange	2	Total Carbohydrate	31 grams
Calories	274	Dietary Fiber	9 grams
Total Fat	6 grams	Sugars	8 grams
Saturated Fat	1 gram	Protein	26 grams
Calories from fat	52	Sodium	387 milligrams

MEAT & VEGETABLE SALADS

BLACK BEAN SALAD

8 servings/serving size: 1 cup

- ◆ 3 cups cooked black beans
- ◆ 2 tomatoes, chopped
- ◆ 2 red peppers, finely chopped
- ◆ 1 cup yellow corn
- ◆ 3 garlic cloves, minced
- ◆ 1 jalapeno pepper, minced

- ◆ 1/4 cup fresh lime juice
- ◆ 2 Tbsp. red wine vinegar
- ◆ 1 Tbsp. cumin
- ◆ 1 Tbsp. olive oil
- ◆ 2 Tbsp. chopped fresh cilantro (optional)

Combine all ingredients and let bowl sit in the refrigerator for several hours to blend the flavors. Serve.

....

Starch/Bread Exchange 1-1/2
Vegetable Exchange 1
Calories 145
Total Fat .... 2 grams
   Saturated Fat .... 0 grams
   Calories from fat 22
Cholesterol .... 0 milligrams
Total Carbohydrate .... 26 grams
   Dietary Fiber .... 7 grams
   Sugars .... 7 grams
Protein .... 7 grams
Sodium .... 77 milligrams

LENTIL SALAD

8 servings/serving size: 1 cup

*T*he flavor of this filling salad improves with time, so you can leave the leftovers in the refrigerator for 2 to 3 days and serve it again!

- 1 lb. dried lentils, washed (rinse with cold water in a colander)
- 3 cups water
- 2 large green peppers, cored, seeded and diced
- 2 large red peppers, cored, seeded and diced

- 3 stalks celery, diced
- 1 red onion, minced
- 2 Tbsp. olive oil
- 2 tsp. cumin
- 1 tsp. minced fresh oregano
- 3 Tbsp. fresh lemon juice
- Fresh ground pepper

1. In a large saucepan over high heat, bring lentils and water to a boil. Reduce the heat to low, cover, and simmer for 35 to 45 minutes. Drain and set aside.
2. In a large bowl, mix together the oil, lemon juice, cumin, oregano and pepper until well blended. Add the lentils and the prepared vegetables. Cover and refrigerate before serving.

....

Starch/Bread Exchange 2-1/2	Cholesterol .... 0 milligrams
Vegetable Exchange 1	Total Carbohydrate .... 38 grams
Fat Exchange 1/2	Dietary Fiber .... 14 grams
Calories 238	Sugars .... 8 grams
Total Fat .... 4 grams	Protein .... 15 grams
Saturated Fat .... 1 gram	Sodium .... 26 milligrams
Calories from fat 40	

COUSCOUS SALAD

3 servings/serving size: 1 cup

Couscous, also known as Moroccan pasta, is very simple to prepare. Place dry couscous in a heat-proof bowl, pour double the amount of boiling water or broth over it and let it sit for 5 to 10 minutes until all the water is absorbed.

- 1 cup couscous, rehydrated (see above)
- 1/4 cup finely chopped red or yellow pepper
- 1/4 cup chopped carrots
- 1/4 cup finely chopped celery
- 2 Tbsp. minced Italian parsley
- 1 Tbsp. olive oil
- 4 Tbsp. rice vinegar
- 2 garlic cloves, minced
- 3 Tbsp. finely minced scallions
- Fresh ground pepper

Combine the couscous and vegetables together in a large bowl. Combine all the dressing ingredients in a blender or food processor and process for 1 minute. Pour over the couscous and vegetables, toss well and serve.

....

Starch/Bread Exchange 2	Cholesterol .... 0 milligrams
Fat Exchange 1/2	Total Carbohydrate .... 32 grams
Calories 191	Dietary Fiber .... 2 grams
Total Fat .... 5 grams	Sugars .... 4 grams
Saturated Fat .... 1 gram	Protein .... 5 grams
Calories from fat 42	Sodium .... 20 milligrams

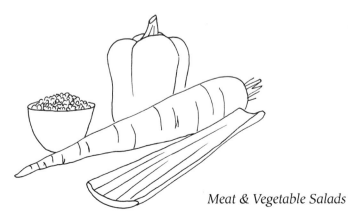

TABBOULEH SALAD

8 servings/serving size: 1/2 cup

You can find the bulgur wheat called for in this recipe in most supermarkets (look in the rice and pasta aisle).

- 1 cup bulgur wheat
- 2 cups boiling water
- 1 large tomato, chopped
- 1/2 cup minced fresh parsley
- 1/4 cup chopped scallions
- 1 Tbsp. chopped fresh mint
- 1/4 cup fresh lemon juice
- Dash salt and pepper
- 1 Tbsp. olive oil
- 1 tsp. ground cumin
- 1 small head butter lettuce
- 1 lemon, cut into wedges

1. In a small bowl, combine the wheat with the boiling water and let stand at room temperature for at least one hour, until the wheat has absorbed the water. The wheat will expand and should yield about 2 cups of rehydrated wheat.

2. Combine the tomato, parsley, scallions and mint with the wheat and toss well. Combine the dressing ingredients together and pour over the wheat salad. Cover and refrigerate overnight or for at least 2 to 3 hours.

3. To serve, place lettuce leaves on individual plates and spoon salad over lettuce leaves. Garnish with lemon wedges.

....

Starch/Bread Exchange	....	1
Vegetable Exchange	....	1
Calories	....	104
Total Fat	....	2 grams
Saturated Fat	....	0 grams
Calories from fat	....	19

Cholesterol	....	0 milligrams
Total Carbohydrate	....	20 grams
Dietary Fiber	....	1 gram
Sugars	....	7 grams
Protein	....	3 grams
Sodium	....	29 milligrams

WILD RICE SALAD

4 servings/serving size: 1 cup

*T*his salad has a slightly sweet flavor.

- 1 cup raw wild rice (rinsed)
- 4 cups cold water
- 1 cup mandarin oranges, packed in their own juice (drain and reserve 2 Tbsp. of liquid)
- 1/2 cup chopped celery
- 1/4 cup minced red pepper
- 1 shallot, minced
- 1 tsp. minced thyme
- 2 Tbsp. raspberry vinegar
- 1 Tbsp. olive oil

1. Place the rinsed, raw rice and the water in a saucepan. Bring to a boil, lower the heat and cover the pan and cook for 45 to 50 minutes until the rice has absorbed the water. Set the rice aside to cool.
2. In a large bowl, combine the mandarin oranges, celery, red pepper, and shallot. In a small bowl, combine the reserved juice, vinegar, thyme and oil. Add rice to the mandarin oranges and vegetables. Pour the dressing over the salad, toss and serve.

••

Starch/Bread Exchange 2-1/2
Calories 205
Total Fat . . . . 4 grams
   Saturated Fat . . . . 1 gram
   Calories from fat 36
Cholesterol . . . . 0 milligrams

Total Carbohydrate . . . . 38 grams
   Dietary Fiber . . . . 5 grams
   Sugars . . . . 7 grams
Protein . . . . 6 grams
Sodium . . . . 22 milligrams

OLIVE AND RICE SALAD

4 servings/serving size: 1 cup

*Y*ou can use white, brown, Italian arborio, or basmati rice in this recipe—experiment until you find your favorite!

- **2 cups cooked rice**
- **3 scallions, chopped**
- **15 Kalamata olives, pitted and chopped**
- **1 green pepper, seeded and diced**
- **1/2 cup chopped red cabbage**
- **3 Tbsp. olive oil**
- **1 Tbsp. red wine vinegar**
- **Dash salt and pepper**
- **1 head romaine lettuce, leaves separated**
- **2 medium tomatoes, quartered**

In a medium bowl, combine the rice, scallions, olives, green pepper and cabbage. Whisk together the oil, vinegar, salt and pepper in a small bowl and pour over the rice salad. Line 4 serving bowls with the lettuce leaves, place salad on lettuce and serve.

....

Starch/Bread Exchange	2	Cholesterol	0 milligrams
Fat Exchange	2	Total Carbohydrate	32 grams
Calories	252	Dietary Fiber	4 grams
Total Fat	13 grams	Sugars	6 grams
Saturated Fat	2 grams	Protein	4 grams
Calories from fat	115	Sodium	327 milligrams

FRESH BROCCOLI SALAD

6 servings/serving size: 1/2 cup

Broccoli is a good source of calcium and Vitamin C.

- 1 lb. fresh broccoli, stems peeled and sliced diagonally, separated into florets
- 1 red pepper, diced
- 1 clove garlic, minced
- 2 Tbsp. red onion, minced
- 1/2 cup red wine vinegar
- 1 Tbsp. olive oil
- 1 Tbsp. chopped fresh chives
- 2 Tbsp. chopped fresh parsley
- 1 tsp. dried basil
- Fresh ground pepper
- 1/2 head romaine lettuce, torn into bite-size pieces

1. Steam the broccoli for 5 minutes. Immediately rinse the broccoli under cold running water to stop the cooking process and help the broccoli retain its bright green color.
2. Add the red pepper, garlic and red onion to the cooled broccoli in a large salad bowl. Combine the rest of the ingredients (except the lettuce) in a small bowl and mix well.
3. Add lettuce to the broccoli mixture and toss. Pour dressing over the salad and serve.

Vegetable Exchange	1	Cholesterol	0 milligrams
Fat Exchange	1/2	Total Carbohydrate	7 grams
Calories	53	Dietary Fiber	4 grams
Total Fat	3 grams	Sugars	4 grams
Saturated Fat	0 grams	Protein	3 grams
Calories from fat	24	Sodium	20 milligrams

GREEN BEAN, WALNUT AND FETA SALAD*

6 servings/serving size: 1/2 cup

*M*ake sure to toast the walnuts—the roasted flavor really enhances this salad.

- 1/2 cup walnuts
- 1-1/2 lb. fresh green beans, trimmed and halved
- 1/2 cup peeled, seeded and diced cucumber
- 1 medium red onion, sliced into rings
- 1/3 cup crumbled feta cheese
- 1/4 cup olive oil
- 1/4 cup white wine vinegar
- 1/4 cup chopped fresh mint leaves
- 1 garlic clove, minced
- 1/2 tsp. salt (optional)

1. Toast the walnuts by placing them in a small baking dish in a 300-degree oven for 10 minutes until lightly browned. Remove from the oven and set aside.
2. Cook the green beans by placing them in a pot of boiling water and then turning off the heat. Do not allow the green beans to boil in the water. Immediately drain and run cool water over the beans to stop the cooking process. This method will help retain their green color and crunchy texture.
3. In a salad bowl, combine the green beans with the walnuts, red onion rings, cucumber and feta cheese. Combine all the dressing ingredients together and toss. Chill 2 to 3 hours before serving.

....

Fat Exchange 3-1/2
Vegetable Exchange 2
Calories 217
Total Fat . . . . 18 grams
   Saturated Fat . . . . 4 grams
   Calories from fat 158
Cholesterol . . . . 11 milligrams

Total Carbohydrate . . . . 13 grams
   Dietary Fiber . . . . 4 grams
   Sugars . . . . 4 grams
Protein . . . . 5 grams
Sodium . . . . 320 milligrams
   w/o added salt . . . . . 142 milligrams

* This salad is relatively high in fat!

WALDORF SALAD

4 servings/serving size: 1 cup

*T*his version of the classic, crunchy fruit salad has less fat and fewer calories.

- ◆ **3 medium kiwi fruit, peeled**
- ◆ **1 large red apple, cored and diced**
- ◆ **1-1/2 cups sliced celery**
- ◆ **1/2 cup plain nonfat yogurt**
- ◆ **1/2 tsp. lemon juice**
- ◆ **1 medium head iceberg lettuce**
- ◆ **12 walnut halves**

1. Cut two of the peeled kiwis into 6 equal wedges and dice the third kiwi. In a medium bowl, combine the kiwis with the apple, celery, plain yogurt and lemon juice.
2. Remove the outer leaves from the lettuce and line 4 individual salad plates to form cups. Spoon apple mixture into each lettuce cup and top with walnut halves. Garnish with 3 kiwi wedges and refrigerate until ready to serve.

....

Fat Exchange	1	Cholesterol	1 milligram
Fruit Exchange	1	Total Carbohydrate	24 grams
Starch/Bread Exchange	1/2	Dietary Fiber	5 grams
Calories	149	Sugars	18 grams
Total Fat	4 grams	Protein	4 grams
Saturated Fat	0 grams	Sodium	70 milligrams
Calories from fat	40		

ITALIAN POTATO SALAD

6 servings/serving size: 1/2 cup

The warm, earthy taste of balsamic vinegar gives this salad its punch. Leave the skins on the red potatoes for a rustic look.

- 24 new red potatoes, 3–4 oz. each, washed and skins left on
- 3 celery stalks, chopped
- 1 red pepper, minced
- 1/4 cup chopped scallions
- 2 Tbsp. olive oil
- 1 Tbsp. balsamic vinegar
- 1/2 Tbsp. red vinegar
- 1 tsp. chopped fresh parsley
- Fresh ground pepper

1. Boil the potatoes for 20 minutes in a large pot of boiling water. Drain and let cool for 30 minutes. Cut potatoes into large chunks and toss the potatoes with the celery, red pepper, and scallions.
2. Combine all the dressing ingredients and pour over the potato salad. Serve at room temperature.

....

Starch/Bread Exchange	1	Cholesterol	0 milligrams
Vegetable Exchange	1	Total Carbohydrate	19 grams
Fat Exchange	1/2	Dietary Fiber	3 grams
Calories	122	Sugars	1 gram
Total Fat	5 grams	Protein	2 grams
Saturated Fat	1 gram	Sodium	29 milligrams
Calories from fat	42		

GREEK POTATO SALAD

10 servings/serving size: 1/2 cup

You'll love this unique potato salad, served warm, with its authentic flavor of Kalamata olives (Greek olives). Find them at your supermarket or a gourmet deli.

- ◆ 1/3 cup olive oil
- ◆ 4 garlic cloves, minced
- ◆ 2 lb. red potatoes, cut into 1-1/2-inch pieces (leave the skin on if you wish)
- ◆ 6 medium carrots, peeled, halved lengthwise and cut into 1-1/2-inch pieces
- ◆ 1 onion, chopped
- ◆ 16 oz. artichokes packed in water, drained and cut in half
- ◆ 1/2 cup Kalamata olives, pitted and halved
- ◆ 1/4 cup lemon juice
- ◆ Dash salt and pepper

1. In a large skillet, heat the olive oil, add the garlic, and saute for 30 seconds. Add the potatoes, carrots, and onion; cook over medium heat for 25 to 30 minutes until vegetables are tender.
2. Add the artichoke hearts and cook for 3 to 5 minutes more. Remove from heat and stir in the olives and lemon juice. Season with salt and pepper. Transfer to a serving bowl and serve warm.

Fat Exchange 1-1/2
Starch/Bread Exchange 1
Vegetable Exchange 1
Calories 177
Total Fat . . . . 8 grams
   Saturated Fat . . . . 1 gram
   Calories from fat 74

Cholesterol . . . . 0 milligrams
Total Carbohydrate . . . . 25 grams
   Dietary Fiber . . . . 4 grams
   Sugars . . . . 4 grams
Protein . . . . 3 grams
Sodium . . . . 237 milligrams

CHINESE CHICKEN SALAD

8 servings/serving size: 3–4 ounces

*T*his is a crunchy salad, loaded with sweet pineapple and crisp water chestnuts.

- 2 cups cooked chicken, diced
- 1 cup finely chopped celery
- 1/4 cup crushed unsweetened pineapple, drained
- 2 Tbsp. finely diced pimentos
- 2 8-oz. cans water chestnuts, drained and chopped
- 2 scallions, chopped
- 1/3 cup low-fat mayonnaise
- 1 Tbsp. lite soy sauce
- 1 tsp. lemon juice
- 8 large tomatoes, hollowed

1. In a large bowl, combine the chicken, pineapple, pimentos, celery, water chestnuts and scallions.
2. In a separate bowl, combine the mayonnaise, soy sauce and lemon juice. Mix well. Add the dressing to the salad and toss. Cover and refrigerate 2 to 3 hours.
3. For each serving, place a small scoop of chicken salad into a hollowed-out tomato. You may also stuff the chicken salad into celery stalks or serve on bread.

....

Lean Meat Exchange 1	Cholesterol . . . . 35 milligrams
* Starch/Bread Exchange 1	Total Carbohydrate . . . . 14 grams
Fat Exchange 1/2	Dietary Fiber . . . . 3 grams
Calories 155	Sugars . . . . 10 grams
Total Fat . . . . 6 grams	Protein . . . . 12 grams
Saturated Fat . . . . 1 gram	Sodium . . . . 196 milligrams
Calories from fat 57	

* Instead of 1 Starch/Bread Exchange, you can use 3 Vegetable Exchanges if you wish.

MEDITERRANEAN CHICKEN SALAD

3 servings/serving size: 3 ounces

Try adding very thin slices of feta cheese to this salad to give it more of a Greek flair!

- 8 oz. boneless, skinless, cooked chicken breast
- 3 Tbsp. olive oil
- 2 Tbsp. balsamic vinegar
- 1/4 tsp. dried basil
- 2 small garlic cloves, minced
- Fresh ground pepper
- 1 cup cooked green beans, cut into 2-inch lengths
- 1/4 cup sliced black olives
- 4 cherry tomatoes, halved

1. Cut the cooked chicken into bite-size chunks and set aside. In a medium bowl, whisk together the oil, vinegar, basil, garlic and pepper. Add the chicken and toss with dressing.
2. Add the green beans, olives and cherry tomatoes; toss well. Refrigerate for several hours. Garnish salad with tomato wedges and serve.

....

Medium-Fat Meat Exchange	3	Cholesterol	67 milligrams
Fat Exchange	1	Total Carbohydrate	7 grams
Vegetable Exchange	1	Dietary Fiber	2 grams
Calories	304	Sugars	3 grams
Total Fat	21 grams	Protein	23 grams
Saturated Fat	4 grams	Sodium	247 milligrams
Calories from fat	186		

SHANGHAI SALAD

4 servings/serving size: 1 cup

Use last night's leftover steak to create this warm Asian salad.

- ◆ 3 Tbsp. canola oil
- ◆ 1 tsp. grated ginger
- ◆ 1 garlic clove, minced
- ◆ 8 oz. cooked lean flank steak, cut into 1-inch pieces
- ◆ 1-1/2 cups fresh snow peas, trimmed
- ◆ 1 8-oz. can water chestnuts, drained and sliced

- ◆ 6 scallions, cut into 2-inch pieces
- ◆ 2 Tbsp. dry sherry
- ◆ 1 Tbsp. lite soy sauce
- ◆ 1 head romaine lettuce, shredded

In a large skillet, heat the oil over medium-high heat. Saute the ginger and garlic for 1 to 2 minutes. Add the remaining ingredients to the skillet and stir until heated through. Arrange shredded lettuce on platter, spoon mixture over the bed of lettuce and serve.

....

Medium-Fat Meat Exchange 2	Cholesterol . . . . 38 milligrams
Vegetable Exchange 2	Total Carbohydrate . . . . 10 grams
Fat Exchange 1-1/2	Dietary Fiber . . . . 3 grams
Calories 267	Sugars . . . . 7 grams
Total Fat . . . . 16 grams	Protein . . . . 18 grams
Saturated Fat . . . . 3 grams	Sodium . . . . 204 milligrams
Calories from fat 148	

DELICIOUS DRESSINGS

BASIC VINAIGRETTE

24 servings/serving size: 1 Tbsp.

- 3/4 cup olive oil
- 3 Tbsp. fresh lemon juice
- 1 garlic clove, minced
- 2 Tbsp. white wine vinegar
- 2 tsp. Dijon mustard
- 1 tsp. minced fresh parsley
- Dash salt and pepper

Combine all ingredients in a blender or food processor. Process until well-blended. Refrigerate until ready to use.

••

Fat Exchange	1-1/2	Total Carbohydrate	0 grams
Calories	61	Dietary Fiber	0 grams
Total Fat	7 grams	Sugars	0 grams
Saturated Fat	1 gram	Protein	0 grams
Calories from fat	61	Sodium	11 milligrams
Cholesterol	0 milligrams		

FRENCH SALAD DRESSING

12 servings/serving size: 1 Tbsp.

This dressing makes a special impression on dinner guests, with its pleasing aroma and pretty color.

- ◆ 1/2 cup olive oil
- ◆ 1/4 cup malt vinegar
- ◆ 1 tsp. salt (optional)

- ◆ Dash lemon pepper
- ◆ Dash paprika
- ◆ 1/4 tsp. dry mustard

Combine all ingredients in a blender or food processor. Process until well-blended. Refrigerate until ready to use.

....

Fat Exchange 2	Total Carbohydrate . . . . 0 grams
Calories 80	Dietary Fiber . . . . 0 grams
Total Fat . . . . 9 grams	Sugars . . . . 0 grams
Saturated Fat . . . . 1 gram	Protein . . . . 0 grams
Calories from fat 81	Sodium . . . . 178 milligrams
Cholesterol . . . . 0 milligrams	w/o added salt . . . . 0 milligrams

GINGER SOY DRESSING

16 servings/serving size: 1 Tbsp.

This dressing can double as a marinade for chicken, turkey or fish.

- 1/2 cup lite soy sauce
- 2 Tbsp. sesame oil
- 2 Tbsp. rice vinegar
- 1 Tbsp. grated fresh ginger
- 1 Tbsp. dry sherry
- 1 tsp. granulated sugar substitute

Combine all ingredients in a small jar, cover tightly, and shake vigorously until well-blended. Keep covered and refrigerated until ready to serve. Shake again before serving.

Fat Exchange 1/2
Calories 20
Total Fat . . . . 2 grams
 Saturated Fat . . . . 0 grams
 Calories from fat 15
Cholesterol . . . . 0 milligrams

Total Carbohydrate . . . . 1 gram
 Dietary Fiber . . . . 0 grams
 Sugars . . . . 1 gram
Protein . . . . 0 grams
Sodium . . . . 300 milligrams

TANGY SALAD DRESSING

12 servings/serving size: 1 Tbsp.

This vegetable-studded dressing also works as a party dip!

- ◆ 1/2 cup low-fat mayonnaise
- ◆ 2 Tbsp. fresh lemon juice
- ◆ 2 Tbsp. white wine vinegar
- ◆ 1 Tbsp. Dijon mustard
- ◆ 2 Tbsp. chopped fresh parsley
- ◆ 2 Tbsp. minced green olives
- ◆ 1 Tbsp. capers
- ◆ 1 Tbsp. minced onion
- ◆ 1 Tbsp. minced celery
- ◆ Fresh ground pepper

Place all ingredients in a food processor and process only until combined. Cover and refrigerate for 1 to 2 hours.

....

Fat Exchange 1/2
Calories 34
Total Fat . . . . 3 grams
   Saturated Fat . . . . 0 grams
   Calories from fat 30
Cholesterol . . . . 4 milligrams

Total Carbohydrate . . . . 1 gram
   Dietary Fiber . . . . 0 grams
   Sugars . . . . 1 gram
Protein . . . . 0 grams
Sodium . . . . 98 milligrams

CREAMY HERB
SALAD DRESSING

24 servings/serving size: 1 Tbsp.

Use *this low-fat, low-calorie creamy dressing over salad greens or as a dip for vegetables.*

- 1/2 cup plain nonfat yogurt
- 1 cup low-fat cottage cheese
- 1-1/2 tsp. fresh lemon juice
- 1 medium carrot, peeled and grated
- 2 tsp. onion, grated

- 1/2 tsp. dried thyme
- 1/4 tsp. marjoram
- 1/4 tsp. oregano
- 1/4 tsp. basil
- 1/4 tsp. salt (optional)

In a food processor, combine the yogurt, cottage cheese and lemon juice; process until smooth. Pour into a small mixing bowl. Add the remaining ingredients and mix well. Cover and refrigerate for 1 to 2 hours before serving.

* Free Food

Calories 11
Total Fat . . . . 0 grams
  Saturated Fat . . . . 0 grams
  Calories from fat 2
Cholesterol . . . . 43 milligrams

Total Carbohydrate . . . . 1 gram
  Dietary Fiber . . . . 0 grams
  Sugars . . . . 1 gram
Protein . . . . 2 grams
Sodium . . . . 64 milligrams
  w/o added salt . . . . . . 43 milligrams

* Remember that only 2 Tbsp. or less is a Free Food!

DILL-FLAVORED
SALAD DRESSING

16 servings/serving size: 1 Tbsp.

*T*ry *this dressing with fresh grilled salmon or swordfish.*

- 1/2 cup plain nonfat yogurt
- 2 Tbsp. low-fat mayonnaise
- 2 tsp. grated onion
- 1 garlic clove, minced
- 1/4 cup skim milk

- 1 tsp. dried dill or 2 tsp. chopped fresh dill
- 1/4 tsp. dried oregano
- Fresh ground pepper

Combine all ingredients in a food processor or blender and process until smooth. Pour into a container, cover and refrigerate for 1 to 2 hours before serving.

....

* Free Food
Calories 10
Total Fat .... 1 gram
   Saturated Fat .... 0 grams
   Calories from fat 5
Cholesterol .... 1 milligram

Total Carbohydrate .... 1 gram
   Dietary Fiber .... 0 grams
   Sugars .... 1 gram
Protein .... 0 grams
Sodium .... 18 milligrams

* Remember that only 2 Tbsp. or less is a Free Food!

PARMESAN SALAD DRESSING

16 servings/serving size: 1 Tbsp.

This dressing also tastes good with cooked broccoli, string beans or asparagus.

- **1/2 cup white wine vinegar**
- **3 Tbsp. grated Parmesan cheese**
- **1 garlic clove, minced**
- **Dash salt (optional)**
- **1/2 cup olive oil**
- **1 tsp. dried basil**
- **Fresh ground pepper**

Place all ingredients in a jar and cover. Shake vigorously and refrigerate until ready to use.

Fat Exchange 1-1/2
Calories 65
Total Fat . . . . 7 grams
   Saturated Fat . . . . 1 gram
   Calories from fat 63
Cholesterol . . . . 1 milligram

Total Carbohydrate . . . . 1 gram
   Dietary Fiber . . . . 0 grams
   Sugars . . . . 1 gram
Protein . . . . 0 grams
Sodium . . . . 26 milligrams
   w/o added salt . . . . . . 18 milligrams

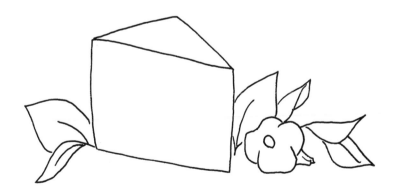

INDEX

DIG INTO OUR *RECIPE-PACKED PANTRY OF COOKBOOKS AND MENU PLANNERS*

Healthy Selects:
Spark Plugs for Your Taste Buds

Dozens of recipes were chosen for each *Healthy Selects* cookbook, but only the 64 most tempting were chosen. Every recipe will fit nicely into your healthy meal plan. Calories, fats, sodium, carbohydrates, cholesterol counts, and food exchanges accompany every recipe.

◆ **GREAT STARTS & FINE FINISHES**

Now you can begin every dinner with an enticing appetizer and finish it off with a "now I'm REALLY satisfied" dessert. Choose from recipes like Crab-Filled Mushrooms, Broiled Shrimp with Garlic, Baked Scallops, Creamy Tarragon Dip, or Cheesy Tortilla Wedges to start; serve Cherry Cobbler, Fresh Apple Pie, Cherry Cheesecake, Chocolate Cupcakes, or dozens of others to finish. Softcover. #CCBGSFF
Nonmember: $8.95/Member: $7.15

◆ **EASY & ELEGANT ENTREES**

Tired of leaving the dinner table feeling like you've had nothing more than a snack? Pull up a chair to *Easy & Elegant Entrees*. Now you can sit down to Fettucine with Peppers and Broccoli, Steak with Brandied Onions, Shrimp Creole, and dozens of others. They taste like they took hours to prepare, but you can put them on the table in minutes. Softcover. #CCBEEE
Nonmember: $8.95/Member: $7.15

◆ **SAVORY SOUPS & SALADS**

Softcover. #CCBSSS. *Nonmember: $8.95/Member: $7.15*

◆ **QUICK & HEARTY MAIN DISHES**

When you're looking for simple, great-tasting meals but can't quite find the time, it's time for *Quick & Hearty Main Dishes*. You'll find Apple Cinnamon Pork Chops, Beef Stroganoff, Broiled Salmon Steaks, Spicy Chicken Drumsticks, Almond Chicken, and many others. Softcover. #CCBQHMD
Nonmember: $8.95/Member: $7.15

◆ **SIMPLE & TASTY SIDE DISHES**

Add a spark of flavor to your main course from four tasty categories of easy-to-prepare sides. In just minutes you can have Herb-Broiled Tomatoes, Sherried Peppers with Bean Sprouts, Brown Rice with Mushrooms, Zucchini & Carrot Salad, Scalloped Potatoes, and dozens of others keeping company with your favorite entrees. Softcover. #CCBSTSD
Nonmember: $8.95/Member: $7.15

The *Month of Meals* series:
Automatic meal planning with a turn of the page

Each *Month of Meals* menu planner offers 28 days' worth of fresh new menu choices. The pages are split into thirds and interchangeable, so you can flip to any combination of breakfast, lunch, and dinner. So no matter which combinations you choose, your nutrients and exchanges will still be correct for the entire day—automatically!

♦ **MONTH OF MEALS**

Choose from Chicken Cacciatore, Oven Fried Fish, Sloppy Joes, Crab Cakes, many others. Spiral-bound. #CMPMOM
Nonmember: $12.50/Member: $9.95

♦ **MONTH OF MEALS 2**

Month of Meals 2 features tips and meal suggestions for Mexican, Italian, and Chinese restaurants. Menu choices include Beef Burritos, Chop Suey, Veal Piccata, Stuffed Peppers, many others. Spiral-bound. #CMPMOM2
Nonmember: $12.50/Member: $9.95

♦ **MONTH OF MEALS 3**

How long has it been since you could eat fast food without guilt? Now you can—*Month of Meals 3* shows you how. Choose from McDonald's, Wendy's, Taco Bell, and others. Menu choices include Kentucky Fried Chicken, Stouffer's Macaroni and Cheese, Fajita in a Pita, Seafood Stir Fry, others. Spiral-bound. #CMPMOM3
Nonmember: $12.50/Member: $9.95

♦ **MONTH OF MEALS 4**

Beef up your meal planning with our "meat and potatoes" menu planner. Menu options include Oven Crispy Chicken, Beef Stroganoff, Cornbread Pie, many others. Spiral-bound. #CMPMOM4
Nonmember: $12.50/Member: $9.95

♦ **MONTH OF MEALS 5**

Automatic meal planning goes vegetarian! Choose from a garden of fresh selections like Eggplant Italian, Stuffed Zucchini, Cucumbers with Dill Dressing, Vegetable Lasagna, many others. Spiral-bound. #CMPMOM5
Nonmember: $12.50/Member: $9.95

♦ **HEALTHY HOMESTYLE COOKBOOK**

Choose from more than 150 healthy new recipes with old-fashioned great taste. Just like grandma used to make—but **without** all that fat. Complete nutrition information—calories, protein, fat, fiber, saturated fat, sodium, cholesterol, carbohydrate counts and diabetic exchanges—accompanies every recipe. Special introductory section features "how-to" cooking tips, plus energy- and time-saving tips for microwaving. Lay-flat binding allows hands-free reference to any recipe. Softcover. #CCBHHS
Nonmember: $12.50/Member: $9.95

☐ **YES!** Please send me the following books:

Book Name: _____ Quantity: _____
Item Number: _____ Total: _____
Price Each: _____

Book Name: _____ Quantity: _____
Item Number: _____ Total: _____
Price Each: _____

Book Name: _____ Quantity: _____
Item Number: _____ Total: _____
Price Each: _____

Book Name: _____ Quantity: _____
Item Number: _____ Total: _____
Price Each: _____

Publications Subtotal $ _____
Virginia residents add 4.5% state sales tax $ _____
Add shipping & handling (see chart) $ _____
Add $15 for each international shipment $ _____
GRAND TOTAL $ _____

Name _____
Address _____
City/State/Zip _____

☐ Payment enclosed (check or money order)
☐ Charge my: ☐ VISA ☐ MasterCard ☐ American Express

Account Number _____
Signature _____
Exp. Date _____ CHA94HS

Shipping & Handling
Up to $30 . . . . .add $3.00
$30.01-$50 . . . . .add $4.00
Over $50 . . . . .add 8%

Mail to: American Diabetes Association
1970 Chain Bridge Road
McLean, VA 22109-0592

Allow 2-3 weeks for shipment. Add $3 for each extra shipping address. Prices subject to change without notice. Foreign orders must be paid in U.S. funds, drawn on a U.S. bank.